SCHA CHRISTMAS

Arranged by
WESLEY SCHAUM and JEFF SCHAUM

CONTENTS

B

THE BLUE BOOK

THE LITTLE DRUMMER BOY

Words and Music by KATHERINE DAVIS,
HENRY ONORATI and HARRY SIMEONE
Arranged by WESLEY SCHAUM

Come they told me pa - rum pum pum pum, _____

A new-born King to see, pa - rum pum pum pum, _____ Our fin - est

gifts we bring pa - rum pum pum pum, _____ To lay be - fore the King pa -

rum pum pum pum rum pum pum pum rum pum pum pum, _____ So to

hon - or Him pa - rum pum pum pum, _____ when we come. _____

HERE WE COME A-CAROLING
(Wassail Song)

TRADITIONAL ENGLISH
Arranged by JEFF SCHAUM

From "Babes in Toyland"

TOYLAND

Lyric by
GLEN MAC DONOUGH

Music by
VICTOR HERBERT
Arranged by JEFF SCHAUM

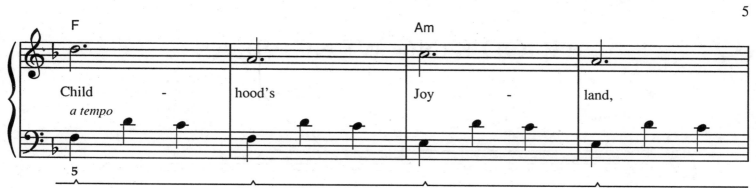

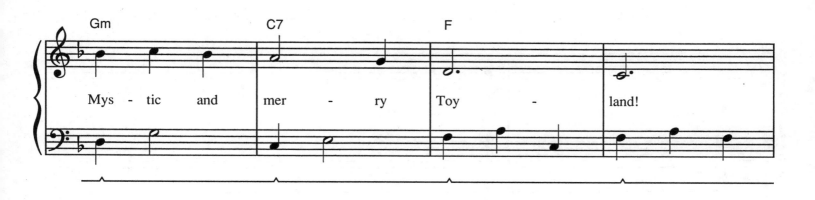

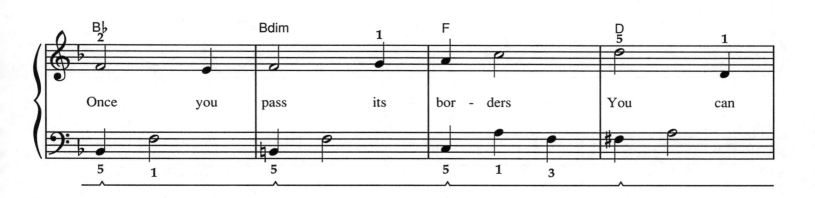

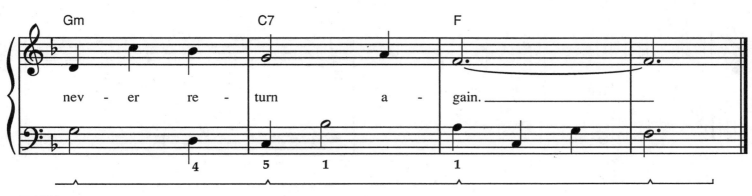

EL03789

GOOD KING WENCESLAS

OLD ENGLISH CAROL
Arranged by WESLEY SCHAUM

COVENTRY CAROL
(Lully, Lullay)

Words by
ROBERT CROO

OLD ENGLISH
Arranged by WESLEY SCHAUM

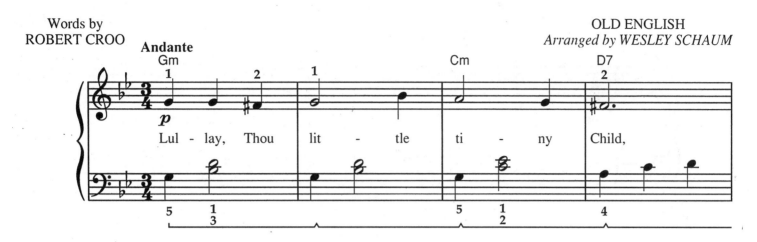

Lul - lay, Thou lit - tle ti - ny Child,

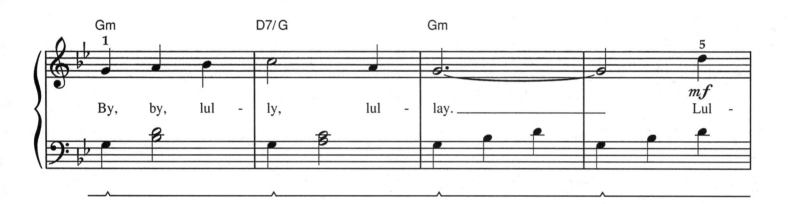

By, by, lul - ly, lul - lay. _____ Lul -

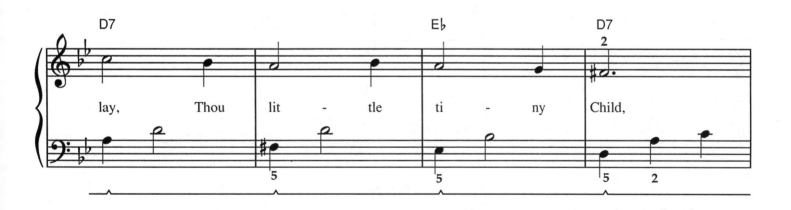

lay, Thou lit - tle ti - ny Child,

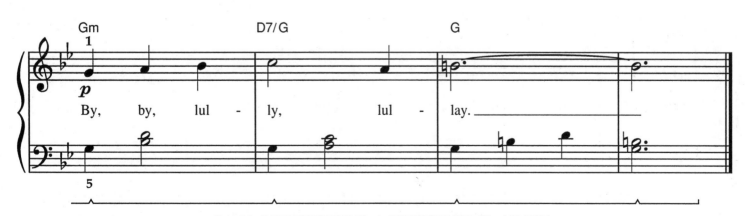

By, by, lul - ly, lul - lay. _____

JOLLY OLD SAINT NICHOLAS

TRADITIONAL
Arranged by JEFF SCHAUM

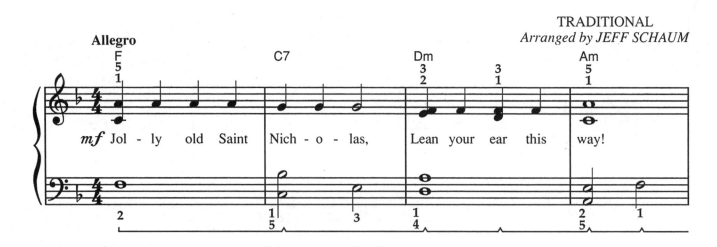

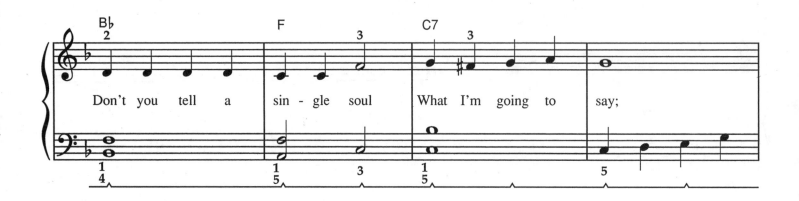

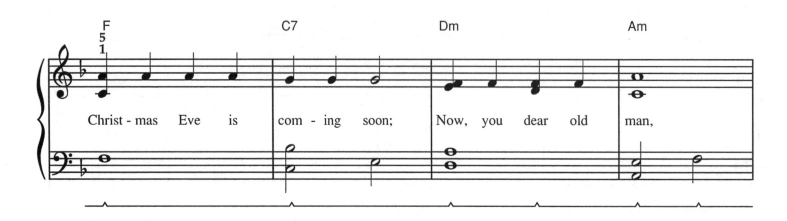

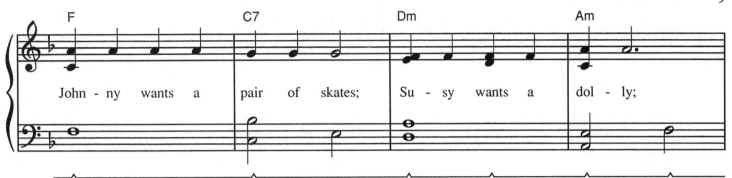

John - ny wants a pair of skates; Su - sy wants a dol - ly;

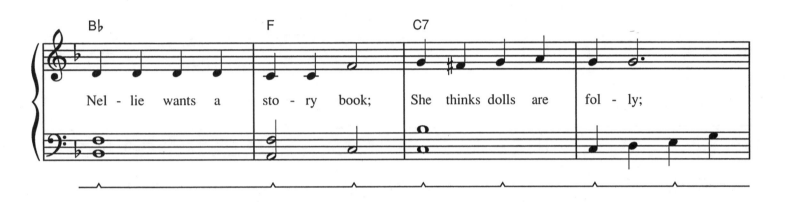

Nel - lie wants a sto - ry book; She thinks dolls are fol - ly;

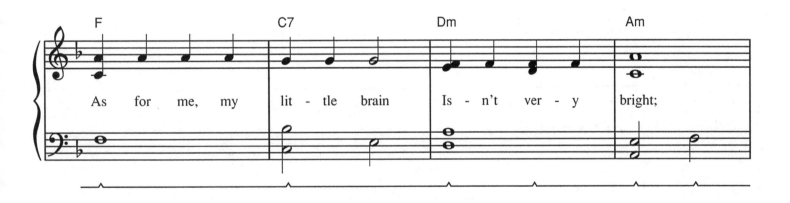

As for me, my lit - tle brain Is - n't ver - y bright;

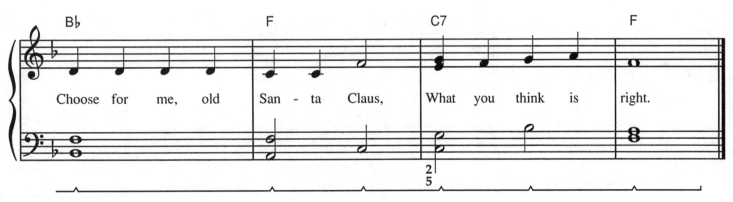

Choose for me, old San - ta Claus, What you think is right.

JOY TO THE WORLD

Words by
ISAAC WATTS

GEORGE F. HANDEL
Arranged by WESLEY SCHAUM

ANGELS WE HAVE HEARD ON HIGH

TRADITIONAL FRENCH CAROL
Arranged by WESLEY SCHAUM

WE THREE KINGS OF ORIENT ARE

J.H. HOPKINS, JR.
Arranged by JEFF SCHAUM

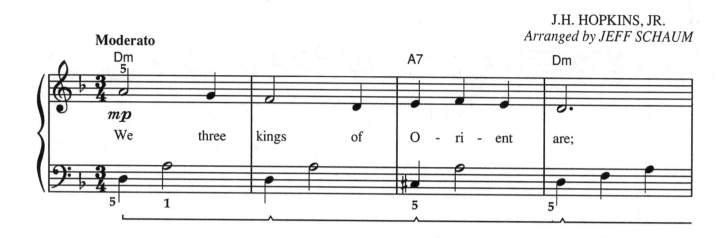

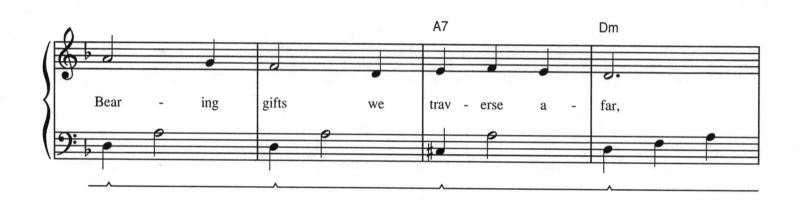

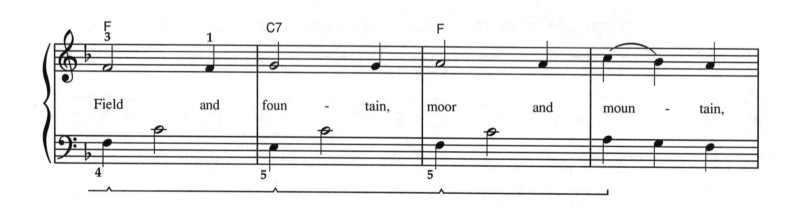

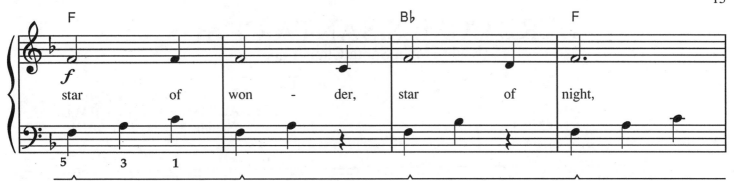

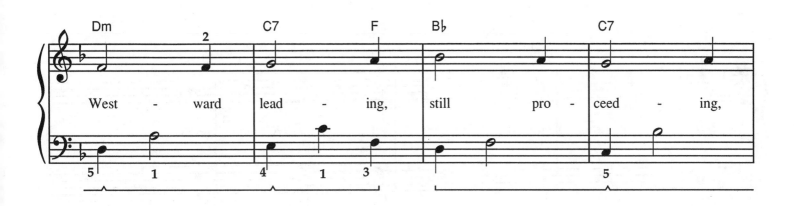

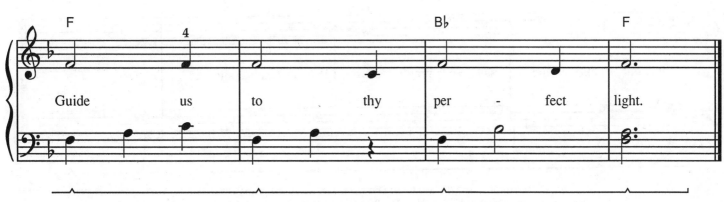

HERE COMES SANTA CLAUS
(Right Down Santa Claus Lane)

Words and Music by
GENE AUTRY and OAKLEY HALDEMAN
Arranged by JEFF SCHAUM

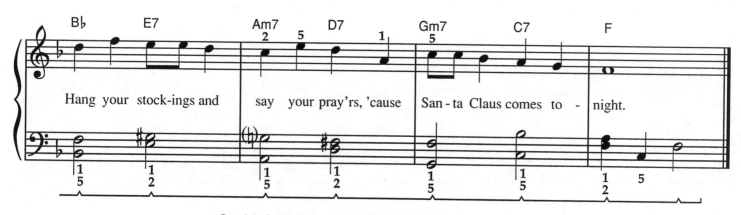

THE FIRST NOEL

TRADITIONAL
Arranged by JEFF SCHAUM

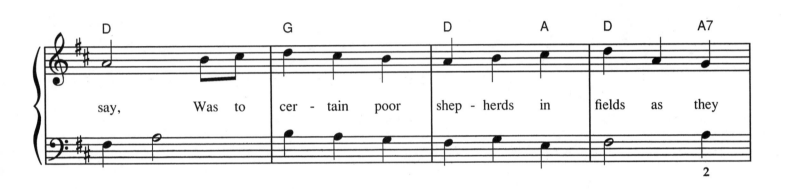

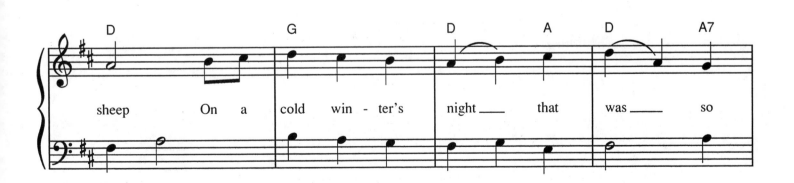

EL03789

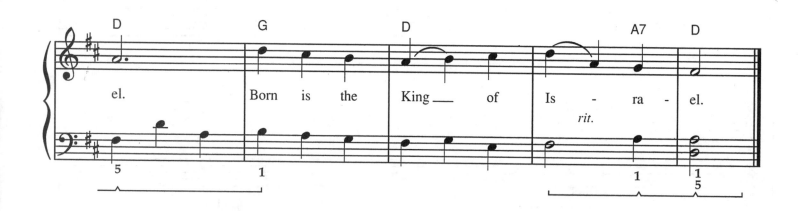

GO TELL IT ON THE MOUNTAIN

SPIRITUAL
Arranged by JEFF SCHAUM

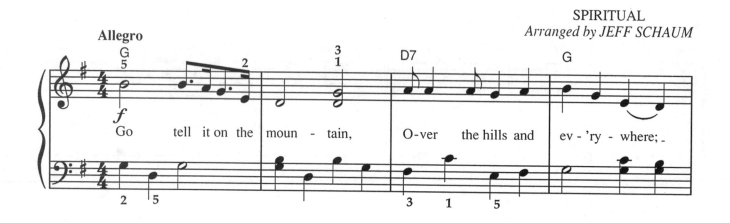

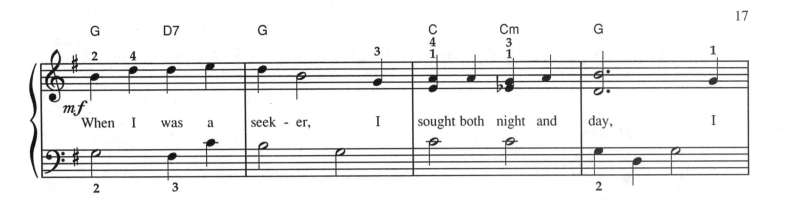

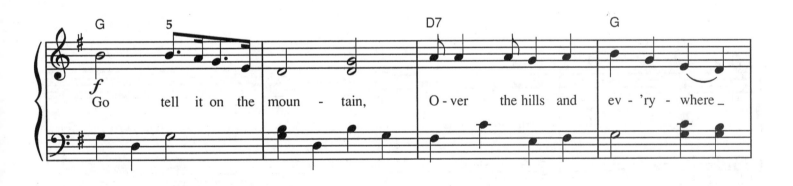

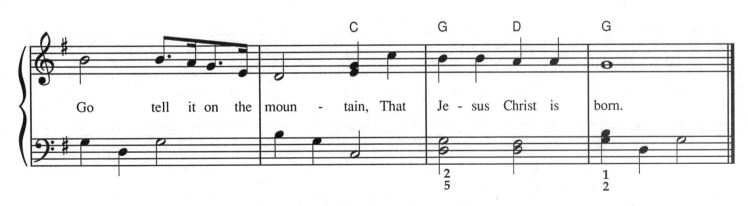

EL03789

LET IT SNOW! LET IT SNOW! LET IT SNOW!

Lyric by
SAMMY CAHN

Music by JULE STYNE
Arranged by WESLEY SCHAUM

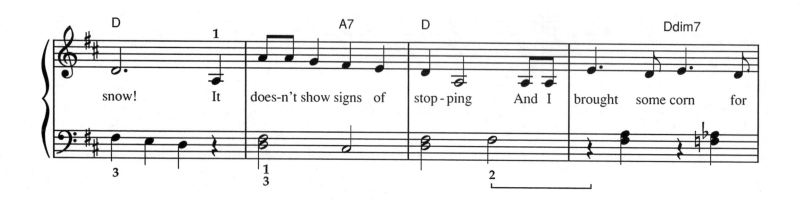

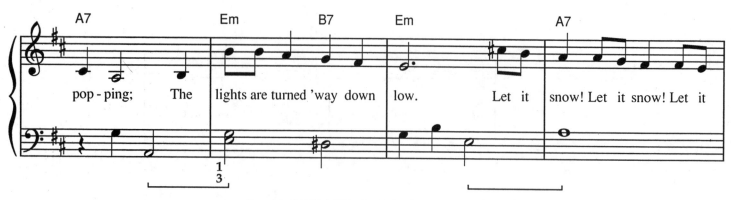

GOD REST YOU MERRY, GENTLEMEN

TRADITIONAL ENGLISH
Arranged by WESLEY SCHAUM

LO, HOW A ROSE E'ER BLOOMING

Words by
THEODORE BAKER

OLD GERMAN HYMN MELODY
Arranged by WESLEY SCHAUM

Lo, how a rose e'er bloom-ing, From ten-der stem hath sprung! Of Jes-se's lin-eage com-ing, As men of old have sung. It came a flow-'ret bright, A-mid the cold of win-ter, When half-spent was the night.

SLEIGH RIDE

Lyric by
MITCHELL PARISH

Music by LEROY ANDERSON
Arranged by JEFF SCHAUM

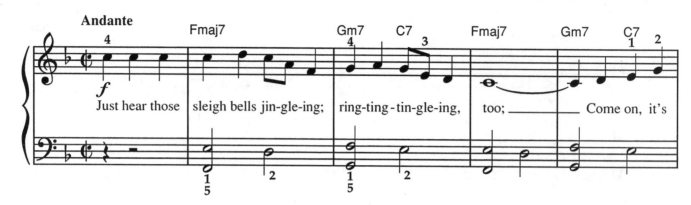

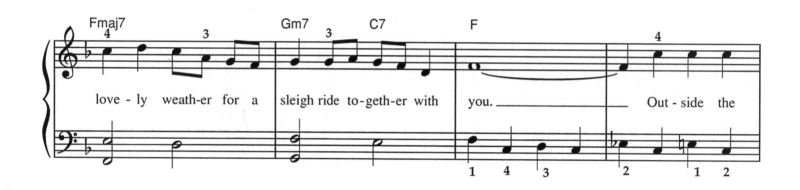

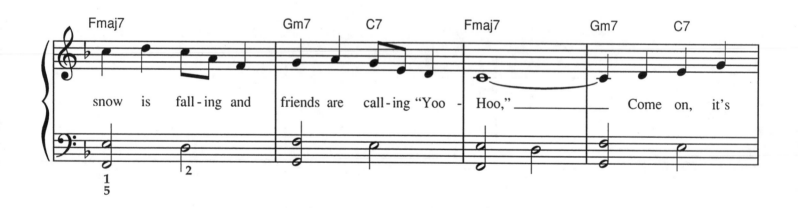

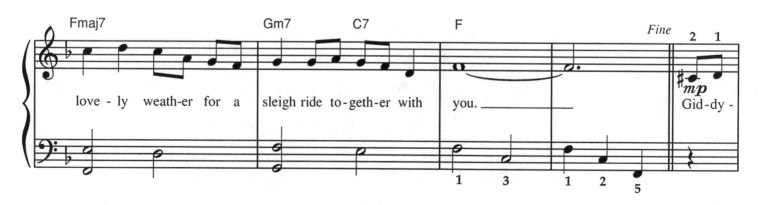

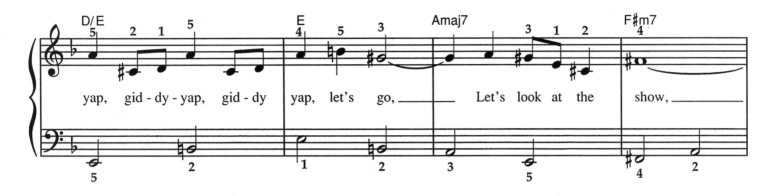

yap, gid-dy-yap, gid-dy yap, let's go, _____ Let's look at the show, _____

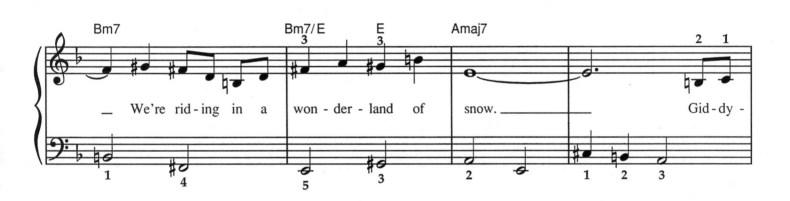

_ We're rid-ing in a won-der-land of snow. _____ Gid-dy-

yap, gid-dy-yap, gid-dy-yap it's grand, _____ Just hold-ing your hand,

D.C. al Fine

We're glid-ing a-long with a song of a win-ter-y won-der-land.

EL03789